D0407717

Christmas 1993

For Mom

Compiled by Jennifer Habel

PETER PAUPER PRESS, INC.
WHITE PLAINS · NEW YORK

FOR MOM:

Because I love you!

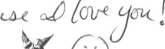 :)

Love,

Mary

*D*ear Mother: I'm all right.
Stop worrying about me.

Papyrus letter of
17-year-old Egyptian girl,
circa 2000 B.C.,
Metropolitan Museum of Art

*B*efore becoming a mother I
had a hundred theories on
how to bring up children.
Now I have seven children and
only one theory: love them,
especially when they least
deserve to be loved.

KATE SAMPERI

The precursor of the mirror is the mother's face.

D. W. WINNICOTT

There are only two things a child will share willingly—communicable diseases and his mother's age.

BENJAMIN SPOCK

Motherhood is being available
to your children whenever
they need you, no matter what
their age or their need.

MAJOR DORIS PENGILLY

Motherhood is a wonderful
thing—what a pity to waste it
on children.

JUDITH PUGH

*Y*ou can choose your friends,
but you only have one mother.
MAX SHULMAN

*M*otherhood affords an instant
identity. First, through
wifehood, you are somebody's
wife, then you are somebody's
mother. Both give not only
identity and activity, but status
and stardom of a kind.
BETTY ROLLIN

I used to be a reasonably careless and adventurous person before I had children; now I am morbidly obsessed by seat-belts and constantly afraid that low-flying aircraft will drop on my children's school.

MARGARET DRABBLE

*E*verybody's mother still cares.

LILLIAN HELLMAN

*I*f you want your children to turn out well, spend twice as much time with them, and half as much money.

ABIGAIL VAN BUREN

*M*otherhood—an incident, an occupation, or a career, according to the mettle of the women.

MARY C. BEASLEY

A mother is a person who if she is not there when you get home from school you wouldn't know how to get your dinner, and you wouldn't feel like eating it anyway.

ANONYMOUS

*W*hat price success if one fails as a mother?

MRS. ROSEMARY FOOT, M.P.

The job description of mother is clearly in need of revision. As it stands, the shifts are twenty-four hours, for a period of approximately 1,825 consecutive days. The benefits are sorely in need of amendment: no vacations, no sick leave, no lunch hours, no breaks. Moreover, it is the only unpaid position I know of that can result in arrest if you fail to show up for work.

MARY KAY BLAKELY

A child without a mother is
like a door without a knob.
JEWISH PROVERB

*L*ove them, feed them,
discipline them and let them
go free. You may have a life-
long good relationship.
MARY G. L. DAVIS

*R*omance fails us—and so do friendships—but the relationship of Mother and Child remains indelible and indestructible—the strongest bond upon this earth.

THEODOR REIK

A woman is her mother.

ANNE SEXTON

*M*y mother loved children—
she would have given anything
if I had been one.

GROUCHO MARX

*S*he was such a good loving
mother, my best friend; oh,
who was happier than I when I
could still say the dear name
"mother," and it was heard,
and whom can I say it to now?

LUDWIG VAN BEETHOVEN

What do you do with mother love and mother wit when the babies are grown and gone away?

JOANNE GREENBERG

Hundreds of dewdrops to
    greet the dawn;
Hundreds of lambs in the
    purple clover;
Hundreds of butterflies
    on the lawn;
But only one mother the
    wide world over.

GEORGE COOPER

*T*he greatest love is a mother's;
then comes a dog's; then
comes a sweetheart.

POLISH PROVERB

"*E*qual parenting" does not
work—the maternal tuning in
never turns off.

PHYLLIS SCHLAFLY

No matter how old a mother is, she watches her middle-aged children for signs of improvement.

FLORIDA SCOTT-MAXWELL

Mothers are fonder of their children than fathers, for they remember the pain of bringing them forth, and are surer that they are their own.

ARISTOTLE

All that I am, or hope to be, I owe to my angel mother.
ABRAHAM LINCOLN

Mom, I love you and I thank you for what you did for me, but I'll never tell you, so I'll have to put it in a song.
GARTH BROOKS,
country music entertainer

*B*ut one thing on earth is better than the wife, and that is the mother.

L. SCHAFER

*G*od could not be everywhere and therefore he made mothers.

JEWISH PROVERB

*I*f the whole world were put
into one scale, and my mother
into the other, the world
would kick the beam.
LORD LANGDALE

I've become a mother. That's
why women grow up and men
don't.
KATHLEEN CLEAVER

*I*n the eyes of its mother every beetle is a gazelle.

MOROCCAN PROVERB

*W*ho ran to help me when
   I fell,
And would some pretty
   story tell,
Or kiss the place to make
   it well?
     My mother.

ANN TAYLOR

*A*ll women become like their mothers. That is their tragedy. No man does. That's his.

OSCAR WILDE

*W*e never make sport of religion, politics, race, or mothers. A mother never gets hit with a custard pie. Mothers-in-law—yes. But mothers—never.

MACK SENNETT

There's more to mothering
than having kids, just as there's
more to being an artist than
owning a paintbrush.

HOLLY NORTH

The hand that rocks the cradle
Is the hand that rules the
world.

W. R. WALLACE

*W*hat the mother sings to the cradle goes all the way down to the coffin.

HENRY WARD BEECHER

*N*ow that I'm pregnant I feel beautiful for the first time in my life.

KAREN ALEXANDER,
fashion model

When a woman is twenty, a child deforms her; when she is thirty, he preserves her; and when forty, he makes her young again.

LÉON BLUM

She never quite leaves her children at home, even when she doesn't take them along.

MARGARET CULKIN BANNING

All most men want from their wives is affection, admiration and the ability to live grandly on an inadequate income.

JOEY ADAMS

My mother had a great deal of trouble with me but I think she enjoyed it.

MARK TWAIN

The mother's heart is the child's schoolroom.

HENRY WARD BEECHER

The patience and the humility of the face she loved so well was a better lesson to Jo than the wisest lecture, the sharpest reproof.

LOUISA MAY ALCOTT,
Little Women

Mother is the name for God in the lips and hearts of little children.

WILLIAM MAKEPEACE THACKERAY

Some are kissing mothers and some are scolding mothers, but it is love just the same, and most mothers kiss and scold together.

PEARL S. BUCK

I think my life began with waking up and loving my mother's face.

GEORGE ELIOT,
Daniel Deronda

*J*udicious mothers will always keep in mind that they are the first book read, and the last put aside, in every child's library.

C. LENOX REMOND

*P*raise the child, and you make love to the mother.

WILLIAM COBBETT

*O*h, to be only half as wonderful as my child thought I was when he was small, and only half as stupid as my teenager now thinks I am.

REBECCA RICHARDS

*T*he mother's face and voice
are the first conscious objects
the infant soul unfolds, and
she soon comes to stand in the
very place of God to her child.
GRANVILLE STANLEY HALL

*B*eing a full-time mother is
one of the highest salaried jobs
in my field, since the payment
is pure love.
MILDRED B. VERMONT

*E*very woman should have a child. The sense of loss must be painful for those without a maternal relationship. There's nothing more warm and sensitive than a child. You complete the full range of emotions. For me, that's what living is all about.

DONNA KARAN

A mother who is really a mother is never free.

HONORÉ DE BALZAC

*W*omanliness means only
motherhood;
All love begins and ends
there—roams enough,
But, having run the circle,
rests at home.

ROBERT BROWNING

*A*sk your child what he wants
for dinner only if he is buying.

FRAN LEBOWITZ

I think most women are scared to death, because we are molding and influencing the most important thing we have ever created, our children. So here we are, sailing out into these totally uncharted waters. And for someone like me, who was trying and wanting to be the very best at everything, there were a lot of anxious, anxious moments.

ANN RICHARDS

*Y*es, a mother is one thing that nobody can do without. And when you have harassed her, buffeted her about, tried her patience, and worn her out, and it seems that the end of the world is about to descend upon you, then you can win her back with four little words. "Mom, I love you!"

WILLIAM A. GREENBAUM II

I always brought up my children not to believe in Mother's Day gifts, and now I regret it.

LAUREN BACALL

*F*ull-time mothering is a tremendously hard job; the heroic women who do it nonstop are to be applauded.

TINA BROWN,
Editor-in-Chief, Vanity Fair

"You agreed to get up nights."
This is true. I stumble into
the nursery, pick up my son,
so small, so perfect, and as he
fastens himself to me like a
tiny, sucking minnow I am
flooded with tenderness.

SARA DAVIDSON

Mother—that was the bank
where we deposited all our
hurts and worries.

T. DEWITT TALMAGE

*M*otherhood has been the most joyous and important experience of my life. I would die for my children.

CARLY SIMON

*I*t is the general rule that all superior men inherit the elements of superiority from their mothers.

JULES MICHELET

A man loves his sweetheart the most, his wife the best, but his mother the longest.

IRISH PROVERB

*W*omen's liberation is just a lot of foolishness. It's the men who are discriminated against. They can't bear children. And no one is likely to do anything about that.

GOLDA MEIR

*I*nstant availability without
continuous presence is
probably the best role a
mother can play.

LOTTE BAILYN

I'm living proof it's possible to
flunk Home Ec, as I did in the
eighth grade, and still be an
outstanding mother.

PAT COLLINS

*I*ntegral to being emotionally healthy is to have a mother who has the ability to respect her child's differences and not perceive them as betrayals. A good mother can allow her child to be less than perfect.

VICTORIA SEGUNDA

*A*ll that I am my mother made me.

JOHN QUINCY ADAMS

*T*he god to whom little boys
say their prayers has a face
very much like their mother's.

SIR JAMES M. BARRIE

*B*eing a "good mother" does
not call for the same qualities
as being a "good" housewife,
and the pressure to be both at
the same time may be an
insupportable burden.

ANN OAKLEY

*W*hat I think I have in common with every mother on the face of the earth is the primacy of one's children in one's life —that they're everything in some bizarre way.

JANE SILVERMAN

*J*ust as you inherit your mother's brown eyes, you inherit part of yourself.

ALICE WALKER

*B*eing a housewife and a mother is the biggest job in the world, but if it doesn't interest you, don't do it. It didn't interest me, so I didn't do it. Anyway, I would have made a terrible parent. The first time my child didn't do what I wanted, I'd kill him.

KATHARINE HEPBURN

*N*ever lend your car to anyone to whom you have given birth.

ERMA BOMBECK

I am the part of the woman
   the same as the man,
And I say it is as great to
   be a woman as to be a man,
And I say there is nothing
   greater than the mother
   of a man.

WALT WHITMAN

If evolution really works, how
come mothers still have only
two hands?

ED DUSSAULT

*W*ith a mother of different
mental caliber I should
probably have turned out
badly. But her firmness, her
sweetness, her goodness were
potent powers to keep me in
the right path. . . . My mother
was the making of me.

THOMAS EDISON

A mother understands what a
child does not say.

JEWISH PROVERB

A mother starts out as the most important person in her child's world and if she's successful in her work, she will eventually become the stupidest.

MARY KAY BLAKELY

*M*otherhood is *not* for the fainthearted. Used frogs, skinned knees, and the insults of teenage girls are not meant for the wimpy.

DANIELLE STEELE

*O*ne of the things I've discovered in general about raising kids is that they really don't give a damn if you walked five miles to school. They want to deal with what's happening now.

PATTY DUKE

*I*t may be said that the most important feature in a woman's history is her maternity.

MRS. TROLLOPE

*E*ven though she's on in years,
she has an enormously
powerful impact on the
children's lives. She is as much
if not more of a presence than
she was when she was more
active. She still has an
indescribable force and time
has not diminished it.

SENATOR EDWARD KENNEDY,
on his mother's 100th birthday

*I*n search of my mother's
garden I found my own.

ALICE WALKER

*F*ive years ago I thought the most courageous thing was not to get married, not to have children. That all seemed so predictable and safe. Now I think the most courageous thing is to get married and *have* children, because that seems the most worthwhile.

CANDICE BERGEN

I think of her, two boys dying of tuberculosis, nursing four others . . . she was a saint.

RICHARD M. NIXON

*M*y mother gave me the example of the completely dedicated life. In my father, this was translated into action, and in my mother into silence. We all live from what woman has taught us of the sublime.

POPE PAUL VI

*O*ne need not be an expert at anagramming to note that MOTHER has much in common with HOME.

KELLY LAKE

The most universal of all truisms is that we all have had a mother. However long or brief that relationship, and however good or bad, there is no disputing that the quality of that relationship is central to our being.

EMILY ROSEN

We bear the world and we make it . . . There was never a great man who had not a great mother.

OLIVE SCHREINER

*O*ne knows one's done one's
job as a parent properly if
one's children reject everything
one stands for.

GLENDA JACKSON

*T*here's nothing particularly
praiseworthy about selling
necklaces at Penney's or writing
memos in an office, over
against the opportunity to
shape a life, to build values, to
show love.

ROBERTA HESTENES,
President, Eastern College

I never thought that you
should be rewarded for the
greatest privilege of life.
MAY ROPER COKER,
1958 Mother of the Year

. . . *b*lest the babe,
Nursed in his Mother's arms,
    who sucks to sleep
Rocked on his Mother's breast,
    who with his soul
Drinks in the feelings of
    his Mother's eye!
WILLIAM WORDSWORTH

*T*he toughest part of motherhood is the inner worrying and
not showing it.

AUDREY HEPBURN

*T*he commonest fallacy among
women is that simply having
children makes one a mother—
which is as absurd as believing
that having a piano makes one
a musician.

SYDNEY J. HARRIS

The future destiny of the child
is always the work of the
mother.

NAPOLEON

Motherhood has a very
humanizing effect. Everything
gets reduced to essentials.

MERYL STREEP

A perfect woman, nobly
    planned
To warn, to comfort, and
    command;
And yet a spirit still, and bright
With something of an angel
    light.

WILLIAM WORDSWORTH,
To Mother

*A*lthough there are many trial
marriages . . . there is no such
thing as a trial child.

GAIL SHEEHY

*M*ost of all the other beautiful things in life come by twos and threes, by dozens and hundreds. Plenty of roses, stars, sunsets, rainbows, brothers and sisters, aunts and cousins, comrades and friends—but only one mother in the whole world.

KATE DOUGLAS WIGGIN

*T*he ideal mother, like the ideal marriage, is a fiction.

MILTON R. SAPIRSTEIN

Because I feel, that in the
   Heavens above,
     The angels, whispering to
   one another,
Can find, among their burning
   terms of love,
     None so devotional as that
   of "Mother,"
Therefore by that dear name
   I long have called you.

             EDGAR ALLAN POE

Men are what their mothers
made them.

      RALPH WALDO EMERSON

*I*n loving memory of my
MOTHER
without whom I might have
been somebody else.
MAE WEST,
dedication of her autobiography

*N*o one knew how deeply I
loved and honored her. Her
death was terrible to me; but I,
once a lord of language, have
no words in which to express
my anguish and my shame.
OSCAR WILDE,
about his mother

No ordinary work done by a man is either as hard or as responsible as the work of a woman who is bringing up a family of small children; for upon her time and strength demands are made not only every hour of the day but often every hour of the night.

THEODORE ROOSEVELT

Mothers have big aprons—to cover the faults of their children.

JEWISH SAYING

*T*he successful mother sets her children free and becomes more free herself in the process.

ROBERT J. HAVIGHURST

*T*he mother-child relationship is paradoxical and, in a sense, tragic. It requires the most intense love on the mother's side, yet this very love must help the child grow away from the mother, and to become fully independent.

ERICH FROMM

*I*f you bungle raising your children, I don't think whatever else you do well matters very much.

JACQUELINE KENNEDY ONASSIS

*Y*et from my earliest days she always had all the love and care I needed; I cannot recall that I ever felt she had been inadequate when my demands on her were emotional rather than practical.

JONATHAN YARDLEY

*F*inally, simply, if I hadn't had a child, I'd never have known that most elemental, direct, true relationship. I don't know if I'd fully understand the values of society that I prize. I would have missed some of the mystery of life and death. Not to know how a child grows, the wonder of a newborn's hand . . . I have been fortunate.

DIANNE FEINSTEIN,
San Francisco Mayor

*M*y mother was dead for five years before I knew that I had loved her very much.

LILLIAN HELLMAN

... *t*hink always that, having the child at your breast, and having it in your arms, you have God's blessing there.

ELIZABETH CLINTON

One good mother is worth a
hundred school masters.

GEORGE HERBERT

To me she was the ultimate
critic. And she was beginning
to think there might be
something to my writing. For
this I was willing to forgive
anything.

LOUIS AUCHINCLOSS

When I broke from modeling,
it felt wonderful because I
stopped thinking of myself as a
pretty face. If I take time off
from acting for motherhood,
my life will deepen in the same
way. I feel as if I've got my
membership now in an
exclusive club and I plan on
enjoying it. Acting can wait.

ANDIE MACDOWELL

The older I become, the more
I think about my mother.

INGMAR BERGMAN

*M*y mother was a wit, but never a sentimental one. Once, when somebody in our house stepped on our cat's paw, she turned to the cat and said sternly, "I *told* you not to go around barefoot!"

ZERO MOSTEL

*T*he finest inheritance you can give to a child is to allow it to make its own way, completely on its own feet.

ISADORA DUNCAN

Who is it that loves me and will love me forever with an affection which no chance, no misery, no crime of mine can do away?—It is you, my mother.

THOMAS CARLYLE

If all mothers want to be demanding or irrational before their children's weddings, I suppose it is their right.

VANESSA L. OCHS

I cannot consent to be separated from my son. I can feel no enjoyment without my children; with them I can regret nothing.

MARIE ANTOINETTE

*F*or the entire five years of my son's life, I have been preparing him to worship the ground I walk on. To date, my crusade hasn't even gotten him to bended knee.

CLAUDETTE RUSSEL

*B*ut the actual power a woman has is to make a group of people happy and make them grow in the right way and contribute to the world. Knowing that you release your family in the morning into the day with your love and with your warmth is the richness of life.

MARIA SCHELL

A mother is a mother still,
  The holiest thing alive.
SAMUEL TAYLOR COLERIDGE

A mother is she who can take the place of all others, but whose place no one else can take.

CARDINAL MERMILLOD

You may despise your mother's leading-strings, but they are the manropes by which many youngsters have steadied the giddiness of youth, and saved themselves from lamentable falls.

HERMAN MELVILLE

A man never sees all that his mother has been to him till it's too late to let her know that he sees it.

WILLIAM DEAN HOWELLS

A suburban mother's role is to deliver children obstetrically once, and by car for ever after.

PETER DE VRIES

*Y*ou can't change your mind—
you know, and say, this isn't
working out, let's sell.

FRAN LEBOWITZ,
on motherhood

*Y*outh fades; love droops,
the leaves of friendship fall:
A mother's secret hope outlives
them all.

OLIVER WENDELL HOLMES

Most children threaten at
times to run away from home.
This is the only thing that
keeps some parents going.

PHYLLIS DILLER

. . . *t*here is nothing so strong
as the force of love; there is no
love so forcible as the love of
an affectionate mother to her
natural child.

ELIZABETH GRYMESTON

*I*f there were no schools to take the children away from home part of the time, the insane asylums would be filled with mothers.

E. W. HOWE

*T*he easiest way to convince my children that they don't need anything is to get it for them.

JOAN COLLINS

*I*t is odd how all men develop the notion, as they grow older, that their mothers were wonderful cooks. I have yet to meet a man who will admit that his mother was a kitchen assassin, and nearly poisoned him.

ROBERTSON DAVIES

*I*s not a young mother one of the sweetest sights which life shows us?

WILLIAM MAKEPEACE THACKERAY

*M*otherhood has relaxed me
in many ways. You learn to
deal with crisis. I've become a
juggler, I suppose. It's all a big
circus, and nobody who knows
me believes I can manage, but
somehow I do.

JANE SEYMOUR

*M*y mother was the most
beautiful woman I ever saw . . .
All I am I owe to my mother.

GEORGE WASHINGTON

With what a price we pay for the glory of motherhood.

ISADORA DUNCAN

My mother is a pretty lady. I wish to kiss her all day but I have to go to school.

TANIA PRICE,
Australian 6-year-old